THE FORTIES

Published by
EMI Music Publishing Limited/Music Sales Limited

Exclusive distributors:
Music Sales Limited, 78 Newman Street,
London W1P 3LA, England.

EMI Music Publishing Limited,
138-140 Charing Cross Road,
London WC2H 0LD, England.

Text Edited by Jonathon Green.
Art Directed by Pearce Marchbank.

Radio Times Hulton Picture Library: Pages 4, 5, 8, 9 and 20
Ken Carroll Collection: Pages 1, 2 and 10

CONTENTS

I WOULD say to this house as I have said to those who have joined this Government: I have nothing to offer but blood, toil, tears and sweat.
— WINSTON CHURCHILL

VICTORY at all costs, victory in spite of terror, victory however long and hard the road may be, for without victory there is no survival.

— WINSTON CHURCHILL

WHEN I go, just skin me and put me on top of Trigger.
— ROY ROGERS

THE cinema, like the detective story, makes it possible to experience without danger all the excitement, passion and desirousness which must be suppressed in the humanitarian ordering ——————— of society.———————
——————CARL JUNG——————

NANCY ASTOR

IF I were your wife I'd put poison in your coffee.

WINSTON CHURCHILL

IF I were your husband, I'd drink it!

NO inanimate thing will move from one place
to another without having a piece of paper
that goes along with it telling someone where to
————— move it. —————
————CHARLES E. WILSON————

I SUPPOSE you have never heard of Karl Marx? He is the other Marx Brother, only they don't recognise him. Nobody knows whether he is funnier or only as funny as they are because ——— no-one understands him. ———
——— **BERNARD BARUCH** ———

MILITARY intelligence is a contradiction in
—————— terms. ——————
——— GROUCHO MARX ———

"Sub Spotted—
LET 'EM HAVE IT!"

COMPARED to war, all other forms of human
endeavour shrink to insignificance. God,
how I love it!
——GEORGE PATTON——

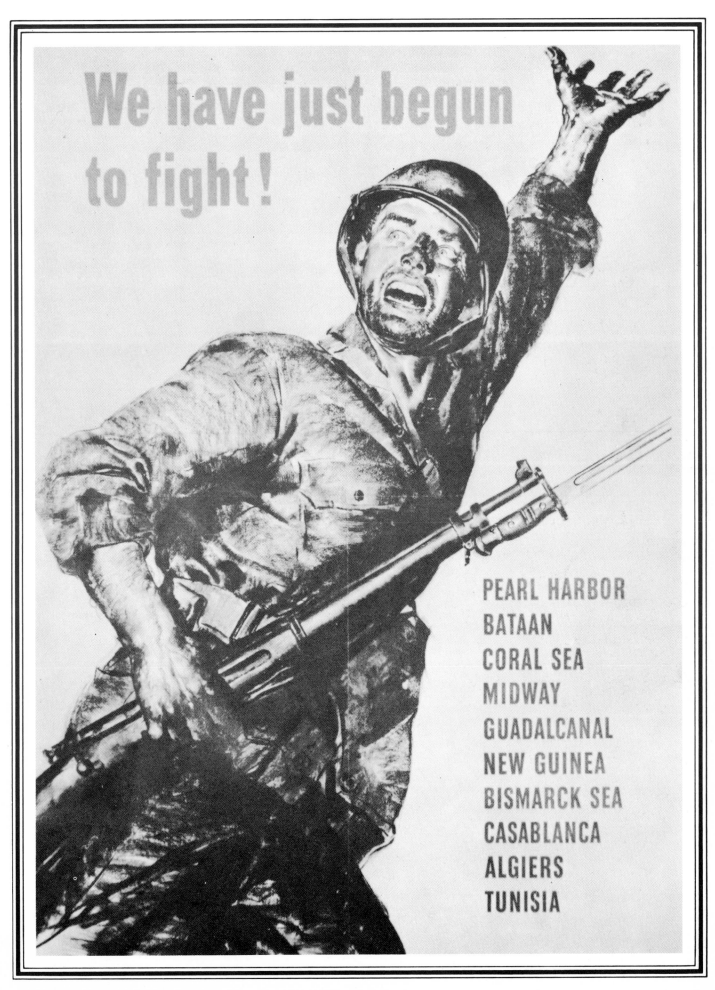

We have just begun to fight !

PEARL HARBOR
BATAAN
CORAL SEA
MIDWAY
GUADALCANAL
NEW GUINEA
BISMARCK SEA
CASABLANCA
ALGIERS
TUNISIA

I CAN sing that sonofabitch off the stage any day of the week.
— FRANK SINATRA —

GIMME a lemonade . . . in a dirty glass.
————— BOB HOPE —————

I HAVE said this before, and I shall say it again: Your boys are not going to be sent into any foreign wars.
— FRANKLIN DELANO ROOSEVELT —

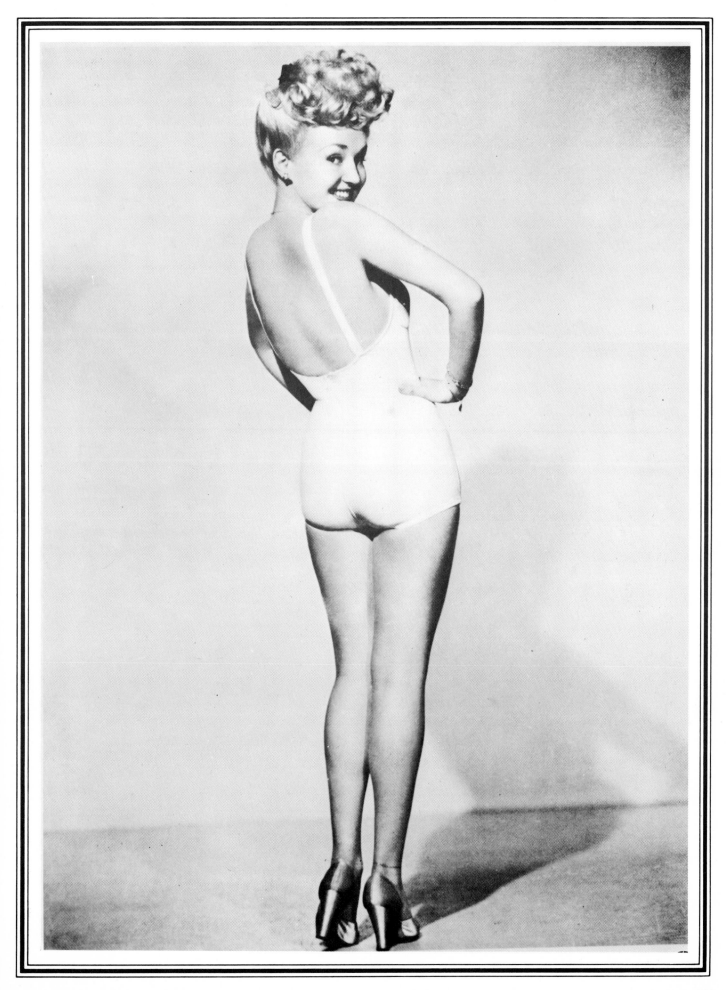

THE war correspondent has his stake – his life – in his own hands, and he can put it on this horse or that horse or he can put it back in his pocket at the very last minute.

——————— ROBERT CAPA, ———————
——— the photographer of this picture ———

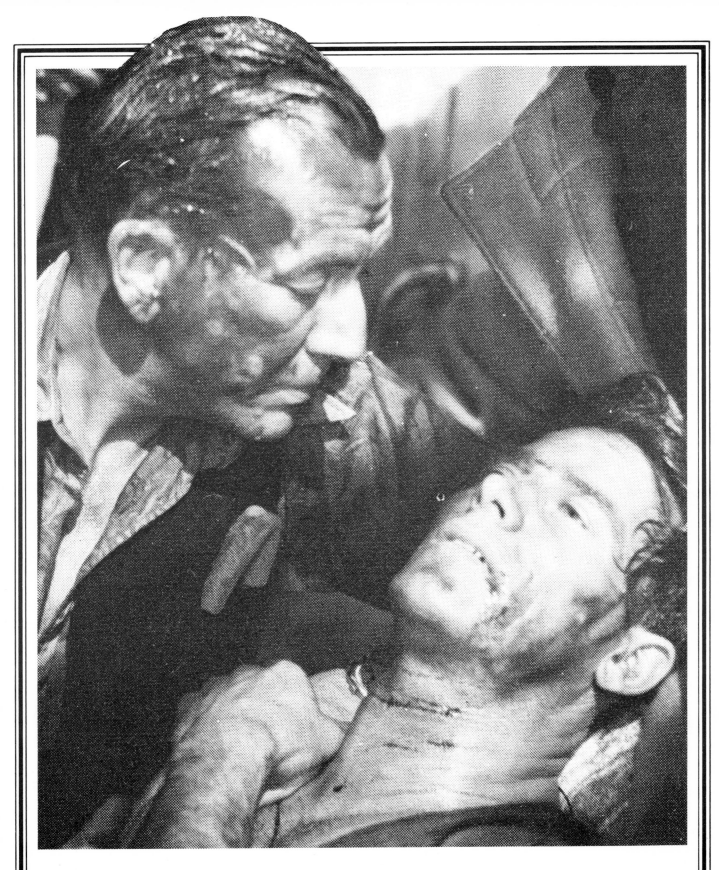

LET us honour, if we can
The vertical man
Though we value none
But the horizontal one.
— W. H. AUDEN, —
—— 'Epigraph' ——

Mind my bike.
_____
JACK WARNER,
catchphrase in
'Garrison Theatre'
_____

This is London . . .
. . . good night,
and good luck.

ED MURROW

I HAVE come to the conclusion that politics are too serious a matter to be left to the politicians.
——————— CHARLES DE GAULLE ———————

I WILL introduce myself: I am Teddy
——— Kennedy's brother. ———
——— JOHN F. KENNEDY ———

BLANCHE DUBOIS

I DON'T want realism, I want magic. Yes, yes, magic! I try to give that to people. I misrepresent things to them. I don't tell the truth, I tell what ought to be the truth. And if that is sinful, let me be damned for it.

TENNESSEE WILLIAMS
Streetcar Named Desire

ACTING is a bum's life – quitting acting,
—— that's a sign of maturity.——
—— MARLON BRANDO ——

AN actor is a guy who, if you ain't talking
—— about him, ain't listening.——
—— MARLON BRANDO ——

I STARTED out very quiet and I beat Mr. Turgenev. Then I trained hard and I beat Mr. de Maupassant. I've fought two draws with Mr. Stendhal and I think I had the edge in the last one. But nobody's going to get me in any ring with Mr. Tolstoy unless I'm crazy or I keep ————— getting better. —————
——— ERNEST HEMINGWAY ———

THE Roller Derby is a sport. Defenestration is also a sport for those who like it.
———— JOHN LARDNER ————

IF I had known, I should have been a locksmith
———— ALBERT EINSTEIN ————

GOD is subtle, but he is not malicious
———— ALBERT EINSTEIN ————

FASCINATION

Words by : Dick Manning
Music by : F. D. Marchetti
Piano Arr. by Ben Pickering

It was FAS-CI-NA - TION I know,............... And it might have end-ed right then at the start............... Just a pas-sing glance,............... ..... Just a brief ro - mance,............... And I might have gone on my way emp-ty

heart - ed........ It was FAS-CI - NA - - TION I know,.......

.... See - ing you a - lone with the moon-light a - bove,.......

.... Then I touched your hand And next mo - ment I kissed you.......

.... FAS-CI-NA-TION turned   to   love................. Then it

love, this was not FAS-CI-NA-TION, I knew As I thrilled to the won-der of you......... It was FASCI - NA - TION I know,......... See-ing you a- -lone with the moon-light a - bove............Then I touched your hand, and next mo-ment I kissed you, ... FASCINATION turned to love.............

YOU'RE NOBODY 'TIL SOMEBODY LOVES YOU

Words & Music by:
Russ Morgan, Larry Stock &
James Cavanaugh

Moderately

Verse

Some look for glo-ry, It's still the old sto-ry Of

love ver-sus glo-ry, And when all is said and done, ___

JEALOUSY

Words by: Winifred May
Music by Jacob Gade

CHORUS

RED ROSES
FOR A BLUE LADY

Words & Music by:
Sid Tepper & Roy Brodsky

CHORUS Moderato

MY HEART AND I

Words by
FRED S. TYSH

Music by
RICHARD TAUBER

Andante

We are in love with you___ My Heart and I,_____ And we are al-ways true,___ My Heart and I,_____ When you are far a-way___ Each smile's a tear_____ But it's a

love-ly day__ When you are near_____ May be that love is blind__ when pas-sion

rules,_____ And that my Heart and I___ are just two fools_____ And yet my

allarg. *ff* *rall. e dim.*

dar-ling, if you ev-er said "Good - bye"_____ I know we both should die__ my Heart and

Moderato *p*

I Once in a life - time a love - dream comes true, Just

Verse may be cut from ✱ to ✱

MY HEART AND I

sempre cresc.

Come what may__ Oh I'll keep smil - ing through, My heart is yours, so you just

f allarg.

take it, It's on - ly ask - ing not to break it!

Tempo I

We are in love with you__ My Heart and I __ And we are

al - ways true__ My Heart and I __ When you are far a - way__ each smile's a

tear____ But it's a love-ly day__ When you are near.____ May be that

Love is blind__ when pas-sion rules____ And that my Heart and I__ are just two

fools,_____ And yet my dar-ling, if you ev-er said "Good-

-bye"_____ I know we both should die,__ My Heart and I!_____

OLD SHEP

Words & Music by: Clyde (Red) Foley

1. When I was a lad, and old Shep was a pup, O'er hills and
2. (So the) years rolled a long, and at last he grew old, His eye-sight was
3. (I) went to his side and sat on the ground, He laid his

mead-ows we'd roam,_____ Just a boy and his dog We were
fast grow-ing dim,_____ Then one day the doc - tor looked
head on my knee,_____ I stroked the best pal that a

both full of fun We grew up to geth-er that way. _____ I re-
at me and said I can't do no more for him, Jim. _____ With a
man ev-er found I cried so I scarce-ly could see. _____ Old

F7　　　　　　　　Bb　Cdim　Bb7　　Eb　　　　Eb7

-mem-ber the time at the old swim-ming hole, When I would have
hand that was tremb-ling I picked up my gun, I aimed it at
Shep-pie he knew he was go-ing to go, For he reached out and

Ab　Eb7　Abm6　　　　Eb

drowned be-yond doubt _____ Shep was right there to the res-cue he
Shep's faith-ful head _____ I just could-n't do it I want-ed to
licked at my hand _____ He looked up at me, just as much as to

Bbdim　　　Bb7　　　Eb　　C7　　　F7

WE'LL KEEP A WELCOME

Words by: Lyn Joshua & James Harper
Music by: Mat Jones

Far a-way a voice is call-ing, Bells of mem-'ry chime "Come home a-gain, come home a-gain," They call thro' the o-ceans of time,____

REFRAIN

We'll keep a wel-come in the hill-side, We'll keep a wel-come in the glen,____ This land you

*We'll keep a wel-come in the hill-sides, We'll keep a wel-come in the vales,____ This land you

*Original Welsh Lyric

knew will still be sing-ing,— When you come home, sweet home a — gain.— There'll be a
knew will still be sing-ing,— When you come home a-gain to Wales.— This land of

friend-ly light to guide you For your re-turn we'll al-ways pray;— We'll kiss a-way each hour of
song will keep a wel-come, And with a love that nev-er fails,— Will kiss a-way each hour of

long-ing When you come home a-gain some day.— We'll keep a   come home a-gain some
☆Hir-aeth, When you come home a-gain   to Wales.— We'll keep a   come home a-gain to

day,—We'll kiss a-way each hour of long — ing When you come home a-gain some day.
Wales.— Will kiss a-way each hour of Hir - aeth, When you come home a-gain to Wales.

☆ Pronounced "Hee-rythe

49

DOWN IN THE GLEN

Words & Music by:
Harry Gordon & Tommie Connor

hea-ven Down in the glen. Though hum-ble it may be, There an an - gel waits for

me In that lone-ly, lit tle hea-ven, Down in the glen. A - cross the moon-lit

hea - ther My las-sie calls as I roam, 'Tis soon we'll be to - ge - ther In that

hea-ven we call "home". The sheep are in the fold And there's peace worth more than

gold, For a shep-herd in that hea - ven Down in the glen. At glen.

LAZY RIVER

Words & Music by:
Hoagy Carmichael & Sidney Arodin

Up a la - zy riv - er where the rob - in's song a-

wakes a bright new morn - ing, We can loaf a - long, Blue skies up a - bove,

ev - 'ry-one's in love, Up a la - zy riv - er, how hap - py you can be,

Up a la - zy riv - er with me.   me.

FRENESI

**English Words by: Ray Charles &
S. K. Russell
Music by: Alberto Dominguez**

CHORUS

MARIA ELENA

English Words by : S. K. Russell
Music & Spanish Lyrics by :
Lorenzo Barcelata

see how much I care?_____ To me your voice is
mor te con sa - gré_____ Mi vi - da la em-be

like the ech-o of a sigh And when you're near, my
lle - ce u na es-pe - ran za a - zul Mi vi - da tie-ne un

heart can't speak a - bove a sigh Ma - ri - a e - le - na Say that
cie - lo que le dis - te tu tu - yo es mi co - ra zon oh

we will nev - er part Ma - ri - a e - le - na Take me
sol de mi que - rer Tu - yo es to - do mi ser tu -

G7   G+   C

Ebdim   Dm   G7

C   Tacet ——— * C

C   Dm   G7   E7

ALWAYS IN MY HEART

Words by: Kim Gannon
Music by: Ernesto Lecuona

Slowly, with expression

There's no moun-tain top so high that some - how love can't climb   No, no, true love will find a way.

There's no riv - er quite so wide That love can't cross in

time. please be - lieve me when I say:

F   F#dim Gm7   G7♭5   C7   Cm7   F7

REFRAIN

You are al - ways in my heart_____ ev - en tho' you're far a -

Bb   F+   Bb   F+7

way,_____ I can hear the mu - sic of_____ the song of

Bb   F+   Bb

love I sang with you._____ You are al - ways in my

E dim   Cm   F7

heart _____ and when skies a-bove are grey_____

I re-mem-ber that you care_____ and then and there the sun breaks

thru. _____ Just be-fore I go to sleep_____

_____ there's a ren-dez-vous I keep_____ and the dream I al-ways

meet _____ helps me for-get we're far a-part, _____

Fm6 G7 Cm

_____ I don't know ex-act-ly when dear _____ but I'm sure we'll meet a-

Ebm6

gain dear _____ and my dar-ling till we do _____ you are al-ways in my

Bb Bbdim F7 A F7

1
heart.

2
You are al-ways in my heart. _____

Bb F+7 Bb

GRANADA

English Words by: Dorothy Dodd
Spanish Words & Music by: Agustin Lara

you could speak what a fas-cin-at-ing tale you would tell,_____ Of an
-tar se vuel-ve gi-ta-no cuan-do es pa-ra ti_____ Mi can-

age_____ the world has long for-got-ten,_____ Of an
-tar_____ he-cho de fan-ta-si-a_____ Mi can-

age_____ that weaves a si-lent mag-ic in Gra-na-da to-
-tar_____ flor de me-lan-co-li-a que yo te ven-go a

sfz

a tempo

-day._____ The
-dar._____ Gra-

f   f   mf

still can be found in the hills all a - round as I
sue - ño re - bel - de y gi - ta - na cu - bier - ta de
wan-der a-long En -
flo - res Y
-tranc'd by the beau - ty be - fore me, En - tranc'd by a
be - so tu bo - ca de gra - na ju - go - sa man-
land full of sun - shine and flow - ers and song. And
-za - na que me ha - bla de a - mo - res Gra-
D.S. al ⊕ Coda

CODA

For soon it will wel-come the stars while a thous-and gui-
De ro-sas de sua-ve fra-gan-cia que le dic-ran

-tars play a soft hab-an-er-a___ Then moon-lit Gra-na-da will
mar-co a la Vir-gen mo-re-na___ Gra-na-da tu tie-rra es-tá

Broadly

live a-gain_ the glo-ry of yesterday ro-man-tic and gay.___ The
lle-na___ de lin-das mu-je-res, de san-gre y de sol.___ Gra-

1

gay.___
sol.

2

70

PERHAPS, PERHAPS, PERHAPS

English Words by: Joe Davis
Spanish Words & Music by: Osvaldo Farres

-HAPS; _____ A mil-lion times I've asked you, and then I ask you
ZAS; _____ Ya-sí pa-san los dí - as_ y yo de - ses-pe-

ov - er_ a - gain, You on-ly an - swer PER - HAPS, PER-HAPS, PER-
-ra - do_ y tú, tú con-tes - tan - do_ QUI - ZAS, QUI - ZAS, QUI-

-HAPS; _____ If you can't make your mind up,_ we'll nev - er get
ZAS; _____ Es - tús per-dien-doel tiem - po_ pen - san - do,_ pen-

start - ed;_____ And I don't want to wind up,_ be - ing
-san - do;_____ Por lo que mas tú quie - ras_ has - ta

part - ed,_ bro - ken heart - ed;_____ So, if you real - ly
cuan - do,_ has - ta cuan - do;_____ Ya sí pa - san los

mp—mf

B7 E Tacet

love me,_ say "yes," But if you don't, dear,_ con -
dí - as_ y yo de - ses - pe - ra - do_ y

Em Am6 B7 Em

-fess, And please don't tell me,_ PER - HAPS, PER-HAPS, PER -
tú, tú con - tes - tan - do_ QUI - ZAS, QUI-ZAS, QUI -

Am6 B7 Em B7 Em B7

1
-HAPS. You won't ad-mit you
-ZAS. Siem-pre que te pre -

mf *mf*

2
-HAPS._____
-ZAS._____

f

Em Am6 B7 Tacet Em Am6 Em

YOU BELONG TO MY HEART

English Words by: Ray Gilbert
Spanish Words & Music by: Agustin Lara

YOU BE-LONG TO MY HEART now and for ev-er
So-la-men-te-u-na vez a-méen la vi-da;

And our love had its start not long a-go
so-la-men-te-u-na vez y na-da más

We were gath-er-ing stars while a mil-lion gui-tars played our love song;
U-na vez na-da más en mi huer-to, bri-lló la es-pe-ran-za,
Y cuan-do-se mi-la-gro rea-li-zael pro-di-gio dea-mar-se;

PERFIDIA

English Words by: Milton Leeds
Music & Spanish Lyric by: Alberto Dominguez

Moderato con espressione

Strangers, and we were sweethearts for so long; Lov-ers, un-til you let your love go wrong.
Na-die com-pren-de lo que su-fro yo can-to pues ya no pue-do so-llo-zar

Kiss me, then give your heart to some-one new; Dar-ling, this is our last a-dieu.
So-lo tem-blan-do de an-sie-dad es-toy to-dos me mi-ran y se van.

I SHOULD CARE

Words & Music by: Sammy Cahn
Axel Stordahl & Paul Weston

I SHOULD CARE, I should go a-round weep-ing;

I SHOULD CARE, I should go without sleep-ing;

Strange-ly e-nough I sleep well, 'Cept for a dream or two;

But, then, I count my sheep well, Fun-ny how sheep can lull you to sleep. So,

BRAZIL

Words by: S. K. Russell
Brazilian Samba by: Ary Barroso

YOU ARE MY SUNSHINE

Words & Music by:
Jimmy Davis & Charles Mitchell

CHORUS

DEEP IN THE HEART OF TEXAS

Words by: June Hershey
Music by: Don Swander

*(Clap Hands)

like per - fume, / yip - pee - yi",   Clap Clap Clap Clap   Deep in the heart of / Deep in the heart of

Tex - as;   Re - minds me of the / The dog - ies bawl, and

Clap Clap Clap Clap   one I love, / bawl and bawl,   Deep in the heart of / Deep in the heart of

1. Tex - as. / Tex - as.   The   2. Tex - as. / Tex - as.

A NIGHTINGALE SANG IN BERKELEY SQUARE

Words by: Eric Maschwitz
Music by: Manning Sherwin

When true lov-ers meet in May-fair, So the leg-ends tell. Song birds sing Win-ter turns to Spring. Ev-'ry wind-ing street in May-fair, falls be-neath the spell I know such en-chant-ment can be, 'cause it hap-pened one eve-ning to me.

That cer-tain night, the night we met, there was mag-ic a-broad in the air There were
strange it was, how sweet and strange, there was nev-er a dream to com-pare With that

an-gels din ing at the Ritz, And a night-in-gale sang in Ber———k'ley
ha-zy, cra-zy night we met, When a night-in-gale sang in Ber———k'ley

Square.   I may be right, I may be wrong, but I'm
Square.   This heart of mine, beat loud and fast, like a

per-fect-ly will-ing to swear, That when you turn'd and smil'd at me, A
mer-ry-go-round in a fair, For we were danc-ing cheek to cheek, And a

night-in-gale sang in Ber———k'ley Square.
night-in-gale sang in Ber———k'ley Square.

The moon that ling-ered ov-er Lon-don Town, poor puzz-led moon, he wore a frown,
When dawn came steal-ing up, all gold and blue, to in-ter-rupt our ren-dez-vous,

How could he know we two were so in love, The whole darn' world seemed up-side down, The
I still re-mem-ber how you smiled and said, "Was that a dream, or was it true?" Our

streets of Town were paved with stars, it was such a ro-man-tic af-fair, And as we kiss'd and
home-ward step was just as light as the tap-danc-ing feet of As-taire, And like an ec-ho

said "good-night" A night-in-gale sang in Ber——k'ley Square. How
far a-way, A night-in-gale sang in Ber——k'ley

Square. I know 'cause I was there, That night in Ber-k'ley Square.

rall

93

ALMOST LIKE BEING IN LOVE

Words by: Alan Jay Lerner
Music by: Frederick Loewe

CLOPIN CLOPANT

French Words by : Pierre Dudan
Music by : Bruno Coquatrix
English Words by : Kermit Goell

CHORUS (*with a slow lilt*)

I go a-long Clo-pin Clo-pant, Whisp'ring "She's gone, she's gone, she's gone" My child-ish heart cries like a
Et je m'en vais Clo-pin Clo-pant, Dans le so-leil et dans le vent—De temps en temps le coeur chan

ba-by—With-out my love—what will each day be?—So I go on Clo-pin Clo-pant, Trudg-ing a-
-cel-le Y'a des souv'nirs—qui s'a-mon-cel-lent—Et je m'en vais Clo-pin Clo-pant, En pro-me-

-long Clo-pin Clo-pant—Love is a dance—and one must learn it—I had my chance—why did I
-nant mon coeur d'en-fant—Com-me s'en-vole—une hi-ron-del-le La vie s'en-fuit—à ti-re

spurn it?—What can I do——but car-ry on? Go-ing a-long Clo-pin Clo-pant. I go a-pant.
d'ai-le—Ca fait si mal——au coeur d'en-fant, Qui s'en va seul, Clo-pin Clo-pant. Et je m'en-pant.

97

COMING IN
ON A WING AND A PRAYER

Words and Music by : Harold Adamson
and Jimmy McHugh

1. O-ver the dim lit flare path an
2. Lis-ten-ing watch-ing hop-ing was

an-xious si-lence reigned, Scanning the blue ho-ri-zon our
all that we could do, Wait-ing for J. for Jim-my and

anx-ious eyes were strained. The ra-di-o sets were hum-ming, they
all the gal-lant crew. Then o-ver our long-ing vis-ion a

wait-ed for a word; Then a voice broke through the humming and
dim grey shad-ow fell, And, like mus-ic, came the mes-sage that

C   F7   C dim C E dim   G7

Chorus **Moderato**

this is what they heard. "Com-in' in on a wing and a
told us all was well.

E dim G7   C7   C7   F   Bb

pray'r _____ Com-in' in on a wing and a

F   Bb   F   Bb   F

pray'r _____ Though there's one mo-tor gone, we can

G7   G7(5b)   C7   F Bb F F7

99

air _____ Look be - low, there's our field o - ver

there _____ With a full crew a - board and our

F   Bb   F   Bb   F

G7   G7(5b)   C7   F   Bb   F   F7

trust in the Lord We're com-in' in on a wing and a

Bb   D dim   C7   F   Bb

pray'r."   "Com - in' pray'r." _____

F   C dim   C7   F   F
                                            Bb

CHATTANOOGA CHOO-CHOO

Words by : Mack Gordon
Music by : Harry Warren

sylvania station 'bout a quarter to four, read a magazine and then you're in Baltimore, Din-

F   C7   F   Gm7 C7   F   C7   F   F9

-ner in the diner nothing could be finer than to have your ham-'n eggs in Carolina. When

Bb   F dim   F   D7   G(9b)   Abm6/C   C9

you hear the whistle blowin' eight to the bar Then you know that Tennessee is not very far, Shov-

F   C7   F   Gm7 C7   F   C7   F   F9

-el all the coal in, gotta keep it rollin' Woo, Woo, Chattanooga there you are.

Bb   F dim   F   D7(+5) D7   G(9b)   C7   F   G7

There's gonna be a certain party at the

C   C dim   C6

103

HEART OF MY HEART

Words and Music by: Ben Ryan

CHORUS Moderato *(with feeling)*

Heart of my heart, I love that mel - o - dy,

Heart of my heart brings back a mem-o- ry, When we were

kids on the cor- ner of the street, We were rough and read-y guys, But

ELMER'S TUNE

Words and Music by: Elmer Albrecht,
Sammy Gallop and Dick Jurgens

1 El - mer ___ de - cid - ed that he would write a lit - tle mel - o - dy; ___
2 Moz - art ___ with - out an - y doubt a - way from all this care and strife ___

Yes sir, ___ he fin - ished it soon and now they're sing - in' El - mer's tune. ___
Knows that ___ he nev - er turned out a tune like this in all his life. ___

CHORUS Moderato *with rhythm*

Why are the stars al - ways wink - in' and blink - in' a - bove? What makes a fel - low start thinking of fall - in' in love? It's not the

sea - son, the rea - son is plain as the moon; It's just El - mer's tune. What makes a la - dy of eight - y go

HOW GREEN WAS MY VALLEY

Music by : Abner Silver
Words by : Benny Davis

I'LL CLOSE MY EYES

Words and Music by: Billy Reid

Eyes_____ If you should pass me by_____ With some-one else_____ may-be who loves you too,_____ I may be lone - ly, But when I see the moon to-night— I'll Close My Eyes, And make be - lieve it's you._____ I'll Close My you._____

LAURA

Words by: Johnny Mercer
Music by: David Raksin

CHORUS Slowly *(with expression)*

Lau - ra ___ is the face in the mist - y light ___ Foot - steps ___ that you hear down the hall ___ The laugh ___ that floats on a sum - mer night ___ That you can nev - er quite ___ re - call ___

LILLI MARLENE

Words and Music by: Hans Leip,
Norbert Schultze and Tommie Connor

Un-der neath the lan-tern by the bar-rack gate, Dar-ling I re-member the way you used to wait;'T was
Time would come for roll call, time for us to part, Dar-ling I'd caress you and press you to my heart; And

There that you whis-pered ten-der-ly, That you lov'd me, You'd al-ways be,
There 'neath that far off lan-tern light, I'd hold you tight, We'd kiss "Good-night,'' My Lil-li of the

lamp-light, My own LIL-LI MAR-LENE.

Or-ders came for sail-ing some-where o-ver there, All con-fined to bar-racks was
Rest-ing in a bill-et just be-hind the line, Ev-en tho' we're part-ed your

more than I could bear; I knew you were wait-ing in the street, I heard your feet, But
lips are close to mine; You wait where that lan-tern soft-ly gleams, Your sweet face seems, To

could not meet; My Lil-li of the lamp-light, My own LIL-LI MAR-
haunt my dreams,

-LENE.

1   Last time

MOONLIGHT SERENADE

Words by: Mitchell Parish
Music by: Glenn Miller

MY GUY'S COME BACK

Words by : Ray McKinley
Music by : Mel Powell

Some - thin's cook-in' that'll rate an ov - a - tion, Will you note that I am in a state of e - la-tion, Won't you

call the press in,'cos I've got a quo - ta-tion And I'll tell the Na-tion That MY GUY'S COME BACK.

time we're steppin' out we real-ly get groovin', And the life's im-prov-in', For MY GUY'S COME BACK. Tell that

Preach-er man to - day is the day

Got my fea-ture man

And we're on our way, Hal - le - lu - jah for MY GUY'S COME BACK.

124

PAPER DOLL

Words and Music by: Johnny S. Black

gone a-way and left me just like all dolls do. I'll tell you boys it's tough to be a-

-lone and it's tough to have a doll that's not your own.

I'm thru with all of them, I'll nev-er fall a-gain,'Cause this is what I'll do.___

CHORUS
Slowly

I'm goin' to buy a PAPER DOLL that I can call my own, A doll that oth-er fel-lows can-not steal, And then the

NOW IS THE HOUR

Words by : Maewa Kaihau
Music by : Clement Scott

Andante molto espress.

1. *Now   is   the   hour*
2. *I'll   dream   of   you*
3. *Ha   -   e   re   ra*

When   we   must   say   good - bye;
If   you   will   dream   of   me;
Te   ma   -   nu   ta   -   ngi   pai;

Soon you'll be sail - ing Far a - cross the
Each hour I'll miss you Here a - cross the
E hae - re a - na, Koe ki pa - ma -

C   C6   Gdim   G   Em   A7

sea. _____ While you're a - way _____ O
sea. _____ It's not good - bye _____ It's
mao. _____ Ha - e - re ra, _____ Ka

D7   G   C   Cm6   G

please re - mem - ber me, _____ When you re
just a sweet a - dieu, Some day I'll
ho ki mai a - no, _____ Ki te

D7   G   C   C6   Gdim

- turn you'll find me wait - ing here. _____
sail a - cross the seas to you. _____
tau E ta - ngi a - tu nei. _____

cresc.

dim.

G   E7   A7   D7   G

129

OUR LOVE AFFAIR

**Words and Music by: Arthur Freed
and Roger Edens**

THE BREEZE AND I

Words by: Al Stillman
Music by: Ernesto Lecuona

Moderato

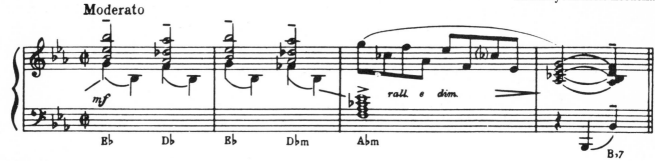

REFRAIN

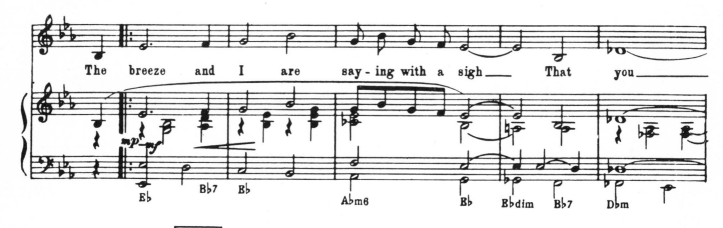

The breeze and I are say-ing with a sigh___ That you___

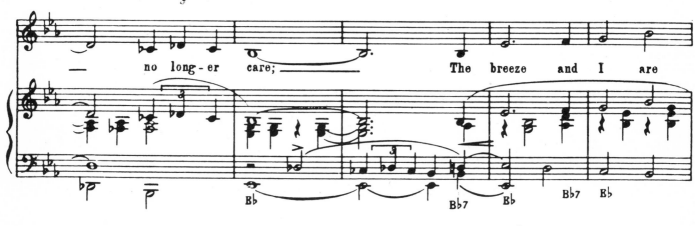

___ no long-er care;___ The breeze and I are

whis-per-ing good-bye___ to dreams___ we used to share.___

THE WHITE CLIFFS OF DOVER

Words by: Nat Burton
Music by: Walter Kent

YOURS

Words by: Jack Sherr
Music by: Gonzalo Roig

This night has mu - sic The sweet-est mu - sic, It ech-oes some - thing with-
The cloak of eve - ning is wrapp'd a - round us, There is a spell in its

- in my heart! ____ I hold you near me, Oh dar - ling hear me,
mys - tic blue! ____ This won - drous eve - ning The moon has found us,

[1] I have a mes - sage I must im - part ___ The cloak of
It hears me of - fer my all to

[2] you ___

YOURS till the stars lose their glo-ry!___ YOURS till the birds fail to sing!___ YOURS to the

Eb   Ebdim Ab Eb   C7 Fm

end of life's sto-ry,___ This pledge to you, dear,___ I oring!___ YOURS in the grey of De-

Fm7 Bb7 Ab Fm7 Bb7   Eb   Ebdim

-cem-ber___ Here or on far dis-tant shores!___ I've nev-er loved an-y-one the way I love

Ab   Eb   Eb7 C7   Fm C7   Fm   Fm7 Bb7 Eb   Eb7 dim

you! How could I?   When I was born to be   just YOURS!___   YOURS!___

Fm C7   Fm   Abm   Eb   Bb7 Eb   Bb7   Eb   137

THE GIPSY

Words and Music by : Billy Reid

REFRAIN

In a quaint car-a-van there's a la-dy they call THE GIP-SY_____ She can
look in the fu - ture, and drive a-way all your fears_____ Ev-'ry-
thing will come right if you on-ly be-lieve THE GIP-SY_____ She could
tell at a glance__ that my heart was so full of tears_____ She

looked at my hand and told me my lov-er was al-ways true, And yet in my heart I

knew dear Some-bo-dy else was kiss-ing you, But I'll go there a-gain 'cause I

want to be-lieve THE GIP-SY That my lov-er is true and will come back to me some

day. In a day.

Ain't Misbehavin' – Ain't She Sweet – Ain't That A Grand And Glorious Feeling
Am I Wasting My Time On You – Among My Souvenirs – Babette
Baby Face – Carolina Moon – Charmaine – Chicago
Dinah – Don't Bring Lulu – Five Foot Two, Eyes Of Blue
Girl Of My Dreams – Glad-Rag Doll – Happy Days And Lonely Nights
I Can't Give You Anything But Love – I'll Be With You In Apple Blossom Time – I'm Just Wild About Harry
It Had To Be You – Last Night On The Back Porch – Manhattan
Mistakes – My Blue Heaven – Nobody's Sweetheart
Pasadena – Ramona – Second Hand Rose
Shine – Side By Side – Singing In The Rain
S'posin' – Stumblin' – Sweetheart Of All My Dreams
That's My Weakness Now – Toot Toot Tootsie! (Goo'Bye) – Way Down Yonder In New Orleans
When You're Smiling – Who's Sorry Now? – You Were Meant For Me

THE Depression Decade. It started with dole queues and ended with marching columns. But throughout those grim years, people never stopped singing. These are some of their favourite tunes. The Nineteen Thirties were tough, but they were always tuneful.

A Bench In The Park – A-Tisket A-Tasket – Auf Wiedersehen My Dear
Back To Those Happy Days – Basin Street Blues – Between The Devil And The Deep Blue Sea
Blue Moon – Careless Love – Exactly Like You – For All We Know
Harbour Lights – Have You Ever Been Lonely? – I Can Dream Can't I?
Ida! Sweet As Apple Cider – I Only Have Eyes For You – I Surrender, Dear
It Happened In Monterey – It's Foolish But It's Fun – Lady Of Spain
Lazybones – Little White Lies – Love Is The Sweetest Thing
Lovely Lady – Lullaby Of Broadway – Marta
Memories Of You – Mood Indigo – Once In A While
On The Sunny Side Of The Street – Red Sails In The Sunset – Serenade In The Night
So Deep Is The Night – Song Of The Dawn – Sophisticated Lady
Star Dust – Stormy Weather – Sweet and Lovely – The Clouds Will Soon Roll By
When It's Sleepy Time Down South – Who's Taking You Home To-night?

In spite of the aftermath of the War, the Nineteen Fifties was a decade of progress, from the austerity that launched the era to the 'Never Had It So Good' slogans at its close. And the music too marked a change which is still prominent today. The Fifties began with the age of the Crooner, but by the middle of the decade a new mood was emerging – the birth of Rock 'n' Roll.

A Beautiful Friendship – Allentown Jail – All The Way
Am I That Easy To Forget? – An Affair To Remember – Answer Me
Autumn Concerto – The Bridge Of Sighs – Cara Mia
Catch A Falling Star – C'est Si Bon – Cry – Ebb Tide
Eternally – Fly Me To The Moon – From A Jack To A King
Green Door – High Noon – Hi-Lili, Hi-Lo
If I Had A Hammer – In The Wee Small Hours Of The Morning – Jailhouse Rock
Kisses Sweeter Than Wine – Love Is A Many-Splendoured Thing – Love Me Tender
Milord – Non Dimenticar – Oh! My Pa-Pa
Passing Strangers – Peggy Sue – Rave On
Release Me – Secret Love – (Love Is) The Tender Trap
Three Coins In The Fountain – Too Young – Unforgettable
Volare – Whisper While You Waltz – Wonderful, Wonderful Day

Printed in Great Britain by
Lowe & Brydone Printers Limited, Thetford, Norfolk